Night Sky and Day Sky

written by Anne Giulieri

Look up into the night sky.

At night time, the sky is black.

On some nights,
you can see lots of stars.
They are a long way up in the sky.
They look like tiny lights.

But on some nights,
you can't see any stars at all.
They are behind the clouds.

You can also see the moon up in the sky.

It can look big and round.

It can look very white, too.

But on some nights, the moon
does not look big and round.

All you can see is a tiny bit of the moon.

It looks like a banana!

On some nights, there is no moon at all!

The sky is very, very black.

It is so black, you can't see at all.

You need a light to find your way.

Look up into the sky in the daytime.
But **don't** look at the sun.
In the daytime, you do not need
a light to help you see.

In the daytime, the sky is
light and bright.
On some days the sun is out.
It is not behind the clouds.

On some days you can see
clouds up in the sky.
The clouds can be white and fluffy.
The clouds can be grey.
The clouds can also be big and black.

14

So, you can see that the night sky
is good to look at.
But the daytime sky is good to look at, too.